Oxford Heritage W

CW00482291

Oxford Heritage Walks
On foot from Broad Street

Malcolm Graham *Malcolm Graham* (signature)

Illustrated by Edith Gollnast *Edith Gollnast* (signature)

OXFORD
PRESERVATION
TRUST

www.oxfordpreservation.org.uk

Oxford Preservation Trust

www.oxfordpreservation.org.uk

First published in Great Britain 2014

Illustrations produced by Edith Gollnast
Map produced by Alun Jones
Designed by Nick Clarke

A catalogue of this book is available from the British Library
ISBN 978-0-9576797-1-9

Printed and bound at Holywell Press, Oxford

ALSO IN THE OXFORD HERITAGE WALKS SERIES

Book1: On foot from Oxford Castle to St Giles'

Contents

About Oxford Preservation Trust

Oxford Preservation Trust is a well-established and forward-thinking charity who own, restore and care for land and buildings in the city, its setting and its views. We work hard to conserve and enhance Oxford, to give the public access to it, and to share and encourage an interest in its history. The Trust recognises that Oxford will change and develop over time and seeks to guide and not to stop, this change to Oxford's heritage.

"Oxford is growing. Its growth may be guided but should not be grudged. The work of the Trust is not to hamper Oxford but to help it. The beauty of Oxford is one of the treasures of the world."

Sir Michael Sadler, founder Trustee, OPT Annual Report (1927)

This guide records some of these changes to our beautiful city, filling in the gaps – lost buildings and memories – so that we can make sense of Oxford's rich history, appreciate and enjoy it now and in the future. It offers a reminder of the contribution more modest buildings and features make to our enjoyment of the streetscapes and skyline and their importance to the city as a whole. We are delighted that these Heritage Walks will enable a new audience to get to know and appreciate more about Oxford.

Debbie Dance, Director, 2013

Oxford Preservation Trust would like to thank the Greening Lamborn Trust, CPRE Oxfordshire Buildings Preservation Trust, the Barnsbury Charitable Trust, Mrs Margaret Leighfield and the William Delafield Charitable Trust for their generous donations to this project, Alun Jones for his wonderful map and John Ashdown for his architectural and historical advice.

The Greening Lamborn Trust's objective is to promote public interest in the history, architecture, old photographs and heraldry of Oxford and its neighbourhood by supporting publications and other media that create access to them.

Table of Illustrations

25. Fragments of ceramic internal wall tiles from former Sainsbury's 4 High Street

26. Lamp & sign above main entrance to 'The Mitre', High Street

27. Bears Mural by Hugh Dunford-Wood. Avenue 3

28. Central Cross Avenue roofs

29. Hayman's fish shop, Avenue 1

4 Turl Street to St Mary's Passage

30. Looking east along Brasenose Lane to Radcliffe Square

31. Ducker's shop front, 6 Turl St.

32. Former All Saints' Church now Lincoln College Library

33. Royal Arms above double doors High Street range, Brasenose College

34. Detail of south porch, St. Mary the Virgin Church

35. Memorial to David Gregory, internal South Wall, St Mary the Virgin Church

36. Cast iron pump west of south porch, beneath almond tree at St Mary the Virgin Church

37. Satyrs on porch and green man on door, Brasenose College.

5 Radcliffe Square and Bodleian Library

38. Two heads from All Souls' iron gates facing Radcliffe Square

39. Radcliffe Square glimpsed from the passage to the Schools' Quadrangle

40. Detail of Earl of Pembroke's statue

6 Catte Street to Broad Street

41. Bridge of Sighs, Hertford College

42. 'Annunciation' stone carving, Chapel of Our Lady at Smithgate

43. Two grotesques: Sir Thomas Bodley & 3 Men in a boat (to say nothing of the dog) Bodleian Library

44. Detail of trophy carvings, North elevation Sheldonian Theatre

45. Earl of Clarendon Statue, Clarendon Building

46. Oxford's coat of arms carving, Weston Library

47. Elephant & howdah weather vane, former Indian Institute

48. Hindu god term, former Indian Institute

49. Blackwell's & The White Horse public house Broad St.

50. Door Knocker on Kettell hall, Trinity College

51. Main Iron Gates at Trinity College

52. Three of the Emperors' Heads from the screen wall outside the Sheldonian Theatre & Old Ashmolean

Foreword

This book is the second in the series Oxford Heritage Walks which revisits and expands upon the On Foot in Oxford leaflets and booklets published by Oxford City Libraries and Oxfordshire County Libraries between 1973 and 1988. Twelve of these trails were published in all, two of them being subsequently revised and reissued under variant titles. They were written by Malcolm Graham, Local Studies Librarian for Oxford City until 1974 and for Oxfordshire from 1974. Local artists supplied the drawings, Laura Potter illustrating the first eight trails and Edith Gollnast the others. Edith also provided additional drawings for the two revised booklets. Oxford Preservation Trust gratefully acknowledges copyright permission from Oxfordshire County Council to reuse text and illustrations from these publications.

Like the earlier trails, the Oxford Heritage Walks seek to encourage interest in the history of the City and the evolution of the built environment. They are not primarily guides to Oxford's world-famous architectural treasures for which there are many alternative sources. Rather, they will explore how each area has developed and focus attention especially on streets and buildings of local importance which add character to every corner of our City. They are envisaged as a treasure-chest of information about Oxford and as a veritable arsenal of historical evidence for defending those features which make the City a special place. In support of that role, the text of each walk with full bibliographical references will also be available online at www.oxfordpreservation.org.uk

Author

Malcolm Graham read History at Nottingham University before doing a postgraduate librarianship course in Leeds and an M.A. in English Local History at Leicester University. He came to Oxford in 1970 as the City's first full-time local history librarian and took on the same role for the County in 1974. Between 1991 and 2008, he was Head of Oxfordshire Studies with Oxfordshire County Council. He has published extensively on local history – his first On Foot in Oxford town trail appeared in 1973 - and he has given hundreds of talks and broadcasts over the years. He was awarded a PhD by Leicester University for a study of the development of Oxford's Victorian suburbs and he is a Fellow of the Society of Antiquaries of London. Away from local history, he enjoys walking, cycling, outdoor swimming, music and the theatre. He is married and lives in Botley.

Illustrator

Edith Gollnast studied art and design at Banbury School of Art and architectural conservation at Bristol University. For thirty five years she worked with historic buildings and areas at Oxford City Council. Edith lives in Oxford, where amongst other pursuits she does freelance illustration.

Map produced by Alun Jones

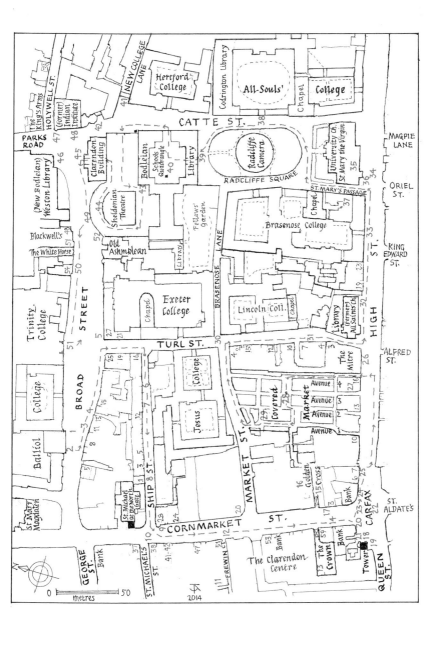

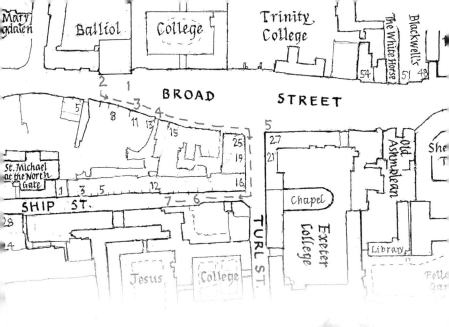

1 Broad Street to Ship Street

The walk begins at the western end of Broad Street, outside the Fisher Buildings of Balliol College (1767, Henry Keene; refaced 1870). 'The Broad' enjoyably combines grand College and University buildings with humbler shops and houses, reflecting the mix of Town and Gown elements that has produced some of the loveliest townscapes in central Oxford. While you savour the views, it is worth considering how Broad Street came into being. Archaeological evidence suggests that the street was part of the suburban expansion of Oxford in the 12th century. Outside the town wall, there was less pressure on space and the street is first recorded as Horsemonger Street in c.1230 because its width had encouraged the sale of horses. Development began

on the north side of the street and the curving south side echoes the shape of the ditch outside the town wall, which, like the land inside it, was not built upon until c.1600. Broad Street was named Canditch after this ditch by the 14th century but the present name was established by 1751.

Broad Street features in national history as the place where the Protestant Oxford Martyrs were burned: Bishops Latimer and Ridley in 1555 and Archbishop Cranmer in 1556. A paved cross in the centre of Broad Street and a plaque on Balliol College commemorate these tragic events. In 1839, the committee formed to set up a memorial considered building a church near the spot but, after failing to find an eligible

1. Martyrs' Cross, set in carriageway

site, it opted instead for the Martyrs' Memorial (1841, Sir George Gilbert Scott) in St. Giles' and a Martyrs' aisle to St. Mary Magdalen Church (1842, Scott & Moffatt).

Until 1772, the width of Broad Street outside Balliol was masked by a forecourt with trees like the one still outside St. John's College in St. Giles'. In 1858, the local architect John Gibbs hatched a plan for a King Alfred fountain in the middle of the street to celebrate the supposed founder of Oxford University. Nothing came of this proposal and the central area became a cab rank and a parking space for market carts. Sarah Angelina Acland led a campaign to build a cabmen's shelter in 1885 and this wooden structure on wheels provided a centrepiece in Broad Street except on occasions when delinquent undergraduates relocated it! A municipal garden was suggested for the site in 1912

but a new cabmen's shelter occupied it instead. In 1928, formal car parking took over the street despite aesthetic objections and a complaint from Parker's bookshop that passers-by would no longer be able to see the shop above car roofs.

The struggle between utility and aesthetics has continued to this day. In 1972, there was talk of bringing Carfax Conduit back from Nuneham Park to the city centre and a full-scale mock-up of the monument was wheeled around Broad Street to see where it would look best. Partial pedestrianization was introduced in 1999 with a movable barrier at the west end of the street, and car parking was briefly banned before being reintroduced east of Turl Street. In 2002, the Oxford Preservation Trust brought together the main interested parties to produce a vision for Broad Street, and Kim Wilkie Associates subsequently produced a report which envisages a pedestrianized University 'Square' outside the refurbished New Bodleian Library. A Luminox event in March 2007, when the entire street was lit up by installations with flaming torches, demonstrated the exciting potential of this great space but Broad Street today remains very much in a state of transition.

Balliol College (founded c.1263) dominates the western end of Broad Street and continues around the corner, northwards into St. Giles'. The Fisher Building was retained when the Master's Lodgings and Brackenbury Buildings (1867–8, Alfred Waterhouse) gave the college a large-scale Gothic façade. Notice the coat of arms of Robert Scott, Master of Balliol, on the Master's Lodgings and, beyond the college entrance, you can see the arms of Hannah Brackenbury who helped to fund the development. Waterhouse's building has not always been popular, and the well-travelled

quote 'C'est magnifique mais ce n'est pas la gare' – it's magnificent, but not the railway station – has been applied to it. The whole façade now has a sense of permanence but, in 1936, the architects Samuel and Harding prepared unrealized plans, which would have replaced the Master's Lodgings with a strikingly modern dining hall.

Town houses on the opposite side of Broad Street provide a foil to Balliol's grand buildings and are best appreciated from here. Development of City-owned land on the site of Canditch began in c.1600 when the population of Oxford was rising swiftly and surviving buildings reflect the narrowness of the original plots, having expanded upwards rather than outwards, like trees in an unthinned plantation. Most of these properties are now listed but, between the Wars, they were seen as outdated and the City became interested in the development potential of the site. Away to your right,

2. Arms of Robert Scott on Master's Lodgings (stars & crescent motifs) & arms of Hannah Brackenbury east of main entrance, Balliol College

nos. Boswell House (1929, North, Robin and Wisdon) was one consequence, replacing several town houses, one of which had been occupied between 1918 and 1922 by the poet, W.B. Yeats and his family. The new building was built in a Classical style for Boswell's department store, founded c.1738 as a trunk-making business, which moved here from Cornmarket Street. By September 1939, the City Council was set to demolish all the other Broad Street houses as far as Turl Street and the return frontage in Ship Street as part of a comprehensive redevelopment scheme that was to include a new City Library, but work was postponed on the outbreak of war and the plan was eventually – and mercifully – abandoned. Older properties begin with nos. 6–8 and 11–13, a series of three and four storey stuccoed houses with sash windows and bands at each floor, which date from the late 18th or early 19th century. No. 6 was home to the Oxford Story attraction between 1987 and 2007, offering visitors a tour through the history of the University in little moving desks. The upper floors of the building have now been converted into student accommodation, a welcome re-use of many city centre houses, and the Ship Street Centre, a Jesus College development (2008–11, Architects' Design Partnership) incorporates a surviving bastion in the city wall. This is sometimes known as the Martyrs' Bastion because Archbishop Cranmer is said to have watched the burning of Bishops Latimer and Ridley from it in 1555.

Set between the stuccoed façades, nos. 9 and 10 Broad Street (1863, William Wilkinson) are of very different character, with red brick, prominent half-timbering and elaborate bargeboards in the gable. Between 1874 and 1895 the shop was occupied by the famous Oxford photographer, Henry Taunt (1842–1922), who had a photographic gallery and workrooms on the upper floors.

Thornton's bookshop, established in Magdalen Street in 1835, attracted generations of bibliophiles to no. 11 Broad Street between 1870 and 2002. All four floors were filled with books until the 1990s and customers could always hope to come away with a real find. Now The Buttery, the building retains a fine 19th century shopfront with thin cast-iron columns. Note the name, Thornton, in the tiled entrance. There is another good shopfront, unfortunately with recently replaced lettering, at no. 13 where the tailors, Castell & Son, have been in business since c.1852. Gillman & Son, a long-established boot-making firm in Oxford, were at no. 12 Broad Street between 1956 and 2002. From at least 1772, no. 12 was the home and studio of John Baptist Malchair (1730–1812), artist and musician. He was born in Cologne and came to England in c.1754, arriving in Oxford in 1759. His drawings of the changing 18th century city are of great importance and he also preserved folksongs that he'd heard sung in the streets. Note the passageway beside no. 13, which formerly led through to Boxall's

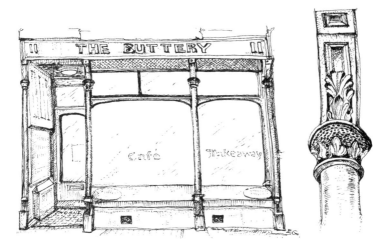

3. 11 Broad Street, 'The Buttery' shopfront

Buildings: more houses packed in behind the street frontage. Henry Taunt had his picture-framing workshop here in the 1870s.

Two mid-18th century houses follow, no. 14 being a four storey house with a stuccoed front dwarfing its three storey neighbour, no. 15, which has been home to Oxford's Visitor Information Centre

4. Portrait of John Malchair, 12 Broad Street

since 2003. Both no. 15 Broad Street and the slightly later no. 16 are of timber-framed construction behind plastered fronts, but nos. 17 and 18 (1868) mark the return to fashion in Victorian times of exposed structural brickwork, adorned here with stone dressings and canted oriel windows above the shopfronts. Following the establishment of the Oxford Famine Relief Committee in 1942, no. 17 became the first Oxfam shop in the country (1948) and the charity's offices until 1962. A blue plaque recalls Cecil Jackson-Cole (1901–79), entrepreneur and philanthropist, who was a founder of Oxfam and helped to set up this shop. Hunt's Office Services occupied no. 18 between 1910 and the 1980s, having begun next door at no. 17 in 1903. Note the Lucy & Co, Eagle Ironworks, Oxford manhole cover outside no. 18.

Continuing east towards Turl Street, we're

back to timber-framed properties with plastered or stuccoed fronts and considerable variation in height. Nos. 19–22 are from the early 18th century with later remodelling. Morton's customers at no. 22 can walk down the side passage to a secluded back garden with views of a converted bastion in the city wall and the backs of Ship Street houses. Nos. 23 and 24 Broad Street are of late 18th century date with canted bays, and a fifth storey was added to no. 23 in the 19th century. No. 25 on the Turl Street corner has a plain front with oval windows beside first and second floor sashes. Bookshops have featured prominently in the history of some of these properties, notably Shrimpton & Son at nos. 23–24 between 1852 and 1901 and Frank Wood at no. 22 between 1929 and 1949. Blackwell's ran the first ever Children's Bookshop at no. 22 between 1950 and 1974 (it was then at no. 6 from 1974 to 1986 and at no. 8 from 1986 to 2002) and opened the Paperback Shop at nos. 23–24 in 1961.

From the corner of Balliol, you have a fine view of the south side of Broad Street beyond Turl Street where University and college buildings have gradually come to dominate the scene since the 17th century. We'll see the major University buildings at the end of the walk and concentrate for now on Exeter College, which occupies the foreground. The college secured a back gate into the street during the 17th century and this proved useful during the notorious county election in April 1754 as a way of getting Whig voters past the Tory roughs armed with bludgeons who were controlling access to the row of polling booths in Broad Street. Exeter only began to build here in 1833–4 when H. J. Underwood built the Gothic range east of the later gate-tower and range by Sir Giles Gilbert Scott (1856). The plain ashlar stone façade of the Thomas Wood Building (1964, Brett and Pollen) occupied a site between Scott's building and Turl Street. Notice, on the roof, a male nude statue (2009, Anthony Gormley), which gazes down nonchalantly at passers-by. Until the 1960s, Barnett House (1889, C.C. Rolfe) stood on this corner of Turl Street; it was a large red brick building originally erected as a private house with consulting rooms and a patient's bedroom for the GP, Dr Julius Ottaway Sankey. Barnett House, a social studies centre, took it over in 1915 and accommodated growing university facilities such as the Tutorial Classes Committee and the Department of Social Anthropology. Well-known local institutions also began there, among them the Oxfordshire Rural Community Council in 1919 and Oxfordshire County Libraries in 1924. Parker's bookshop (established 1798) operated from a late 18th century property next to Barnett House and expanded into the building in 1937. The firm acquired a new split-level shop in the Thomas Wood Building and, since Parker's closed in 1988, Blackwell's Art & Poster Shop has occupied these premises.

5. Anthony Gormley's nude man sculpture on Thomas Wood building, Exeter College. Exeter Chapel fleche to left

Leave Broad Street for the time being and turn right into Turl Street. This is now a simple matter, but pedestrian access through the city wall at this point was only created in c.1550–1. Initially, there was just a hole in the wall and the turnstile or twirling gate, which kept out cattle and carts, gave the street its unusual name. The gateway was demolished in 1722, and the tall stuccoed timber-framed houses on your right were built soon after the road was widened

in 1785. Elmer Cotton's sports shop has flourished at no. 18 since 1910 and its window displays feature quality sports equipment as well as framed photographs of Varsity sporting groups, some more revealing than you might expect! The Taj Mahal, one of the first Indian restaurants in England outside London, opened at no. 16 in 1937. Since 2011, the Hub, a centre for Oxford student volunteers, and the Turl Street Kitchen have occupied nos. 16-17. A mature horse chestnut

6. View east along Ship Street to Exeter College and chapel.

tree on the far corner of Ship Street is a fine sight, particularly in Spring when its 'candles' are in flower. Further on, you can see the Turl Street ranges of Exeter College (founded 1314) on your left and Jesus College (founded 1571) on your right. Both were entirely refaced in Gothic style in the 19th century, Jesus College by H. J. Underwood in 1833–4 and Exeter College by J. C. and C. A. Buckler in 1854. Note the small-sized cut stones characteristic of the period.

Turn right into Ship Street, which was first mentioned in the 12th century. First known as Summoner's Lane in 1385, it had become Ship Lane after the inn at the north-west end of the street by 1772. It formed part of a circuit of roads just inside the city wall but, as the wall became less important for defence, the open land within and the moat outside became potential building sites owned by the city. The eastward continuation of Ship Street vanished when it was leased to Exeter College in 1623 as the site for

7. Ship Street houses and view east to Exeter College and chapel

a new chapel. Notice here the towering fleche of the later chapel (1854–6, Sir George Gilbert Scott), a building modelled loosely on the Saint Chapelle in Paris. West of Turl Street, house-building on the right-hand side of Ship Street began in c.1600 and the existing houses form an attractive group, though – as in Broad Street – they were spared from demolition only by the outbreak of the Second World War. Most are 17th century in origin but they were generally altered or re-fronted to accord with 18th century taste. Stucco was used to mask the timber framing, although jetties are visible on the upper floors of several houses. Sash windows have replaced earlier casements and flat canted bays are evident at no. 11, which has a rare wooden rusticated ground floor as well as a surviving Sun insurance mark above the door. Unfashionable gables were usually displaced but do survive at nos. 10 and 12. Note the Dean & Son, Oxford manhole cover near no. 12's front door. At the far end, nos. 1–5 Ship Street (c.1756) are of different character and were formerly the Ship Inn; they are three storeys high, stone built with attic dormers. A carriage entrance to the inn yard survives between nos. 2 and 3, but it leads now to the Ship Street Centre,

Jesus College accommodation in a former warehouse built for the furniture dealer William Baker (1882, Frederick Codd; converted 2008–11, Architects' Design Partnership). You catch a glimpse of the polychromatic brickwork of Codd's large warehouse through the gap between no. 1 Ship Street and St. Michael at the Northgate Church.

The other side of Ship Street is dominated by the north range of Jesus College (1905–7, R. England), a building in the medieval tradition with gate tower and oriel window and a host of enjoyable gargoyles and grotesques. This range was extended westwards as St. Michael's Mansions (1910–12, R. England) with four gables above and shops below. Then comes a real change of scale, a rubble stone house and shop which dates from the 15th century with two added 17th century gables and renewed mullioned windows above the shop front.

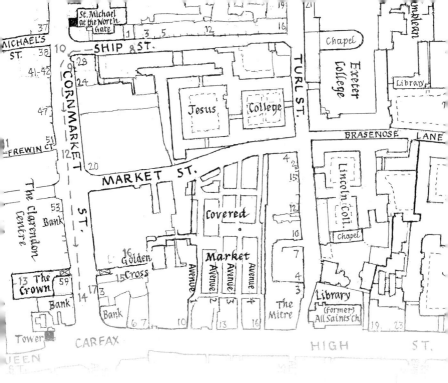

2 Cornmarket Street

oday's bustling Cornmarket Street was originally one of the principal roads of the Saxon *burh*, or defensive town, laid out in c.910 to deter Danish attacks. The North Gate, in the earthen ramparts and, later, stone walls, stood beside the Saxon tower of St Michael at the Northgate Church (c.1020), which vies with St George's Tower at Oxford Castle to be the city's oldest standing structure. The tower is built of Coral Rag stone with 'long and short quoins and two tiers of twin bell-openings with bulgy balusters and through-stones'. A blocked west doorway high up in the tower originally opened onto the adjacent North Gate, which was demolished in 1771. The rest of the church is of 13th–15th century date with the addition of a north transept (1833, John Plowman). Later restoration work by G. E. Street (1853–4) was largely obliterated by a serious fire in 1953.

South of Ship Street, you will see the timber-framed side elevation of no. 28, which the architect Thomas Rayson restored to something like its original appearance in 1951. Together with nos. 26–27, this property has a three-gabled frontage onto Cornmarket Street and it is one of Oxford's few surviving

8. St. Michael at the Northgate Church. Ship Street elevation.

medieval domestic buildings. Built as the New Inn by John Gibbes in c.1390, the property was later subdivided and nos. 26–27 (Pret A Manger) were occupied from the 1870s until 1983 by Zacharias' (estab. 1857), a firm noted for its Wet-Off waterproof clothing. Alterations to the building had left few visible traces of its antiquity but, long after no. 28 was restored, nos. 26–27 were reconstructed along much more archaeological lines (1986, Architects Design Partnership/ John Fryman & F.W. B. Charles) as part of a Jesus College development. It is worth considering going in for a bite to eat and taking the opportunity to view the rich timber detailing. Burger King next door

at nos. 24–25 is another eating place in a tall, stone-fronted building erected for Capital & Counties Bank Ltd. (1904, R.H. Kerr). The door on the left originally led to student rooms on the upper floors. Notice the decorative carved head at each end of the shop front, perhaps part of the original elaborate frontage or, introduced when Fuller's restaurant took over the premises in 1920. Fuller's was a delightful destination for Oxford shoppers until c.1970, noted specially for its iced walnut cake and peppermint lump. The Kardomah restaurant then occupied the premises until 1976.

Across Cornmarket Street, St Michael's

Street is the continuation of the road inside the city walls, and the tapering spire of Wesley Memorial Church (1878, Charles Bell) beautifully terminates the distant view. On the left hand corner, you'll see the gabled 1665 facade of no. 38 Cornmarket Street, now Austin Reed, Ltd. This was the Plough Inn from c.1656 to 1924 and it was reconstructed in 1925 by Thomas Rayson, initially for Dunn's, the hatters; notice the early Sun Insurance fire mark (c.1720) behind the Plough sign. On the other corner, no. 37 Cornmarket Street (c.1860) retains at first-floor level a cast-iron electric lamp bracket with dragon finial (c.1895). Retained when Cornmarket was re-lighted in 1974/5, this bracket was installed when electric street lighting in Oxford was still in its infancy.

Until the 18th century, Cornmarket was known as Northgate Street from the gate in the city wall beside St. Michael's church. The present name recalls the street's former country and market town character; Dr. John Claymond, President of Corpus Christi College, having built in the middle of the street in 1536 a leaden roof supported by stone pillars 'that thereby in wet seasons sacks of corne might be preserved from the violence of the weather'. This structure was demolished during the Civil War in 1644 to provide lead for bullets and timber for military engines. Although 'sample'

10. Projecting sign. Austin Reed & former Plough Inn, 38 Cornmarket

buying gradually replaced the display of complete loads, increasing traffic made the situation very inconvenient for corn dealers and public alike, and off-street facilities were eventually provided – beneath the new Town Hall (1751) and then in purpose-built Corn Exchanges, the first behind the Town Hall (1861, S. L. Seckham; demol. 1893) and the second in George Street (1894–6, H. W. Moore). Some farmers were, however, still to be seen in Cornmarket on market days as late as 1889, opinion being divided 'as to whether the attraction to the old market site is due to the repellent force of the small fee charged for the use of the new Corn Exchange or to the attractive force of the numerous bars and spirit-vaults in the vicinity of Carfax.'

As you head south, Tom Tower still provides a splendid backdrop as it has done since 1681 when Christopher Wren so ingeniously put the finishing touch to Christ Church's 16th century gatehouse. Cornmarket Street itself has changed considerably in that time, first, through the updating and re-fronting of old gabled properties. No. 39 (Timpson's) for example, next to Austin Reed, has a four-storey 19th century front, possibly disguising an earlier core, and no. 40 (Snappy Snaps) is an 18th century re-fronting of a 17th century house. The canted late 18th century style bays of nos. 41–42 (Orange), and no. 23 opposite (the northern part of W H Smith's), also mask 17th century timber-framed buildings. Commercial development in Victorian times introduced more radical change as whole sites were cleared for brand new buildings. Nos. 47–51 on your right (1879–80, Frederick Codd) are a major surviving example of this trend, a four-storey yellow brick block in fashionable Gothic style. Henry Boswell, a trunk and portmanteau maker, promoted this scheme and he occupied nos. 49 and 50. The tailor, Henry Woodward, took no. 51 before moving to High Street in the early 1920s and joining forces with Arthur Shepherd to create Shepherd & Woodward in 1927.

As Oxford's main shopping street, Cornmarket in the 20th century became the preferred stamping ground for multiple retailers and the pace of change accelerated. Woolworths was the first to arrive in 1925, demolishing the Roebuck, formerly one of Oxford's major coaching inns, for a new store – now occupied by Boots – which at least hid discreetly behind an 18th century style frontage. By 1939, Woolworths had acquired the Clarendon Hotel, formerly the Star Inn, for a much larger store, and, although war delayed the inevitable, demolition followed in 1954. It was arguably Oxford's greatest single 20th century loss, changing the whole character of the street, and paving the way for further developments. Clarendon House (1956-7, façade by Lord Holford), was built on the site and remained a Woolworths store until 1983. The frontage in Clipsham and Bladon stone was 'designed to take its place among Oxford buildings' and the top floor was set back to avoid disturbing the scale of the street. Inside, the new store introduced 'Frood', frozen ready-cooked meals, and plastic housewares to the Oxford public.

Marks & Spencer opened a store opposite north of Market Street at no. 20 in 1935 and extended into no. 21 four years later. Northgate House (1963, Lewis & Hickey), a dreary building faced in Portland stone, represented a further huge expansion for M&S, occupying the site of the original store and an attractive jumble of old properties down to Market Street. M&S moved to Queen Street in 1978 after swapping sites with the Oxford & Swindon Co-operative Society Ltd., and the gargantuan store is now subdivided into four shops. River Island broke up the façade with a welcome first floor showroom window in 2011.

Littlewoods store (1964, D. M. C. Ruddick), now occupied by McDonald's, represented another massive and uncompromisingly modern alteration to the street scene. Ironically, it replaced perhaps the finest of Cornmarket's Victorian buildings (1864, William Wilkinson): Venetian Gothic premises built for the high-class grocery firm, Grimbly Hughes, after a fire in 1863. Grimbly Hughes moved to Queen Street in 1961 but closed down for good in 1963.

If these mid 20th century buildings are difficult to ignore, do not let them blind you to other interesting features as you

head for Carfax. On the west side, a blue plaque on the Frewin Court elevation of Clarendon House records that the Oxfordshire Yeomanry was formed nearby at the Star Inn in 1794. Frewin Court leads to Frewin Hall, now student accommodation for Brasenose College but formerly a private house built on the site of St. Mary's College, a monastic college for Augustinian canons founded in 1453. Richard Frewin (1680/1–1761), a respected physician and Camden Professor of History, lived in the house for many years and Edward, Prince of Wales, later Edward VII, stayed here when he was up at Christ Church in 1859–60. Beside the locked gate to Frewin Hall, a more promising one leads into the Oxford Union Society, arguably the best-known debating society in the world. Founded in 1825, the Union acquired a site for a permanent home in St. Michael's Street in 1852. The red brick Gothic style Debating Hall (1857, Benjamin Woodward), now the Old Library, was the first major development, celebrated for the series of Pre-Raphaelite murals depicting scenes from Arthurian legends which were painted by a team of young artists who included Dante Gabriel Rossetti, William Morris and Edward Burne-Jones. William Morris also decorated the ceiling in 1857, restoring it to a modified design in 1875. You can view the Old Library murals and the Union's later Debating Chamber (1878, Alfred Waterhouse) when the Library is open (admission charge). Outside, the original entrance to the Debating

11. Terracotta letters on Oxford Union Society, Frewin Court

Hall is hidden away beyond the modern Gothic Library extension but it is worth seeking out for the relief of King Arthur and His Knights carved by Alexander Munro from Rossetti's design. Returning to Cornmarket Street, note the large initial W for Woolworths and the date 1957 above the entrance to Clarendon House. After Woolworths closed, the building was converted to form part of the Clarendon Centre (1983–4, Gordon Benoy and Partners) and blue hoops initially decorated the sober stone façade. These proved hugely controversial and they disappeared in a later revamp.

Beyond the Clarendon Centre, you're back to Victorian development at nos. 53–4, the left hand half of Barclays Bank, which was built as the Shakespeare Hotel in 1865. The Banbury bank, Gillett's, took over the premises from 1877 until it amalgamated with Barclays in 1919. Barclays then added the right hand half (1922, Alfred Foster), astonishingly to the same design, on the site of the former Twining's grocer's shop, a gabled timber-framed building. Past McDonald's, Crown Yard leads down to the Crown, a pub since at least 1823 and the last to survive in a street which had 15 licensed houses back in the 19th century. Road widening as part of the Carfax Improvement Scheme claimed older properties beyond here in the 1890s. Nos. 59–61 (1890, H.G.W. Drinkwater), now occupied by Moss Bros, was initially the Metropolitan Bank and then became Montague Burton's tailor's shop from c.1928 to 1976. The

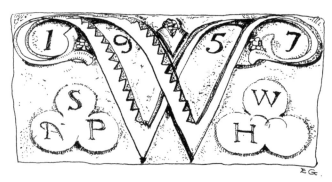

12. 'W' Woolworths initial near Clarendon House entrance

13. The Crown public house Crown Yard

HSBC Bank (1896–7, H.T. Hare) was initially Frank East's drapery store but the building incorporated an archway at the north end leading to the Sun Vaults pub. The Midland Bank had taken over East's by 1914 but the archway – now blocked – provided access to the Carfax Assembly Rooms (J.R. Wilkins) between 1925 and 1966. Many local romances started on the dance floor at this major entertainment venue and the Beatles famously performed here on February 16th, 1963. Back in June 1936, a meeting of Sir Oswald Mosley's Blackshirts was held here and ended in a punch-up.

On the other side of Cornmarket Street, the southern corner of Market Street

14. Two plaster boss fragments of Dragon & Lizard from former Carfax Assembly Rooms (Blocked archway entrance next to the Midland Bank)

15 Golden Cross south range (applied timber framing removed in 1980s refurbishment)

was redeveloped in a neo-Cotswold style (1938–9). Beyond Boots, nos. 6–7 (1907, J. R. Wilkins) are stone fronted with vaguely Dutch gables and have large showroom windows on the first and second floors. They were built for the tailor Arthur Shepherd who occupied no. 7 while the Civet Cat, a toy and fancy goods business, initially took no. 6. The next building along is a 1950s 'curtain wall' re-fronting of the former Weeks' restaurant (1923–4) of which only the top storey survives. It forms a surprising prelude to the Golden Cross, but Oxford's medieval inns and academic halls typically lay behind a fringe of shops, which provided necessary rental income. The Golden Cross, so-named from the 15th century, was owned by New College from 1388 to 1825 and the college arms of chevrons and roses may be seen in a spandrel of the 15th

century entrance gateway. The inn is built around a long narrow courtyard, which may have been used by the King's Players for a performance of Shakespeare's tragedy, Hamlet. The 15th century north range is timber framed and jettied with six original oriel bays on the first floor. The south range is an exuberant later 17th century structure, reflecting the inn's major importance at that time. It is three storeys high with four gabled bays and attics; the upper floors of three bays have original windows with arched centre lights, the so-called Ipswich windows still present in a few 17th century Oxford houses. The 19th century east range is stuccoed, with the ground floor rusticated to imitate large blocks of stone. Pizza Express now occupies the upper floor of the north range and you can enjoy your meal beside meticulously restored

16. Two periods of interior wall painting, North Range, Golden Cross

16th century wall paintings, which include a painted frieze of c.1595 bearing the initials of Pearse and Anne Underhill. Out again in Cornmarket Street, the next property, no. 3, has a plain 18th century front with sash windows and a deep cornice above the modern shop front. Inside, as so often happens, the building is much older, dating from the 15th century and containing elaborate wall paintings in the second floor Painted Room. These are thought to have been commissioned by John Tattleton, a councillor who occupied the house from some time after 1560 until his death in 1581.). Formerly the Crown Tavern, the building was leased to John Davenant, a friend of William Shakespeare, from about 1592 to 1614. Shakespeare regularly stayed at the tavern and was godfather to William Davenant (1606–68), the poet and playwright, who was baptized at St. Martin's, Carfax in 1606. The frontage of the next house south probably dates from the late 18th

And last of the rest be thou

17. Detail of wall painting, 2nd floor, 3 Cornmarket

century but it was radically altered in the early 20th century by the insertion of a showroom window on the first floor: this was perhaps for the hatter, Frederick Margetts, who occupied these premises between c.1914 and 1958. Then comes a narrow half-timbered façade (1876, H.J. Tollit), now part of Lloyd's Bank but originally part of the Jolly Farmers pub.

Walking down Cornmarket Street today, you only need to look out for other pedestrians. This would have been unthinkable when Cornmarket was a busy main road, indeed part of the A34 until the 1960s. The threat that vibration from heavy traffic would destroy Oxford's historic buildings led to the installation of an experimental rubber road here in 1937. When wet, the road became a

virtual skating rink. The experiment was unsuccessful but the rubber blocks were only removed in 1953. With the Oxford ring road completed and attitudes to traffic in towns beginning to change, Cornmarket Street was closed to motor vehicles, apart from buses, in 1973. Particularly after bus deregulation in 1986, the street became noted for its huge bus jams and complete pedestrianization was only achieved in 1999. The street was paved in granite in 2001–2 but, in an echo of the rubber road fiasco, the slabs cracked up and had to be removed. The granite, timber and stainless steel seats, 'designed in such a way that people can't sleep on them', were unveiled to initial incredulity in 2004 but they seem well used today.

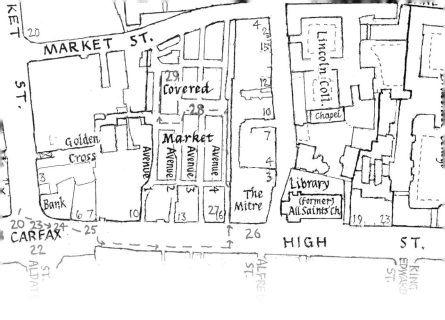

3 Carfax to Covered Market

And so you come to Carfax, which derives its name from the Latin 'quadrifurcus' (four forked) or the Norman-French 'quatre vois' (four ways). The crossroads lay at the heart of the late-Saxon planned town and metaphorically at least it still fulfils this function for today's Greater Oxford. Thomas Hardy's Jude the Obscure spoke of Carfax as having 'more history than the oldest college in the city. It was literally teeming, stratified with the shades of human groups, who had met there for tragedy, comedy, farce; real enactments of the intensest kind …'.

The Town and Gown rioting that began here on St Scholastica's Day, 10 February 1355, was one such enactment with long-term consequences for the history of Oxford. The trouble began at the

Swindlestock Tavern – a plaque on Abbey House marks the site – where a group of scholars began an argument with the landlord, threw some wine in his face and beat him with the empty pot. This dispute quickly escalated into a major battle, which, over three days, led to the deaths of six scholars and an unknown number of townsfolk. (There is no historical evidence for the higher death toll of 63 scholars and around 30 townsfolk which is often quoted.) In the aftermath, the king sided with the university, which received a new charter granting it considerable power in the day to day running of the city. The mayor, bailiffs and sixty citizens were obliged to attend a mass for the souls of the dead at St. Mary's Church each year on St. Scholastica's Day and to swear an oath

The Groundplott of the Conduit

E.G.

18. Penniless Bench & Butterbench. Carfax c 1720

to observe the university's privileges. This humiliating ceremony continued in modified form until 1825 and the mayor's oath until 1859.

St. Martin's Church, first recorded in 1032, was formerly the main focal point at Carfax, terminating views along High Street, and it was very much associated with Town rather than Gown. In 1340, Edward III ordered the church tower – in essence, today's Carfax Tower – to be lowered following complaints from scholars that 'the townsmen would in times of combat with them retire up there as to their castle and from thence gall and annoi them with arrows and stones, etc'. The common bell of the church was an early messaging device, summoning townsmen to the fight on St. Scholastica's Day or advising them of significant events such as a royal visit. St. Martin's became the City Church, its services attended by the Mayor and Councillors, who listened to sermons by a specially appointed City Lecturer. Official business was conducted outside the church, especially around the Penniless Bench, which was built against the east wall of the church in 1545 and survived in various forms until the late 18th century. Penniless Bench was a general meeting place and people seeking work gathered there but, as the name implies, it also became something of a magnet for 'idle and disorderly persons'. Long after the bench had been removed, Carfax remained a place where labourers waited to be hired and members of the so-called 'Carfax Club' continued to annoy respectable folk.

The medieval and later St. Martin's Church was declared unsafe in 1818 and rebuilt (1821–2, John Plowman), leaving only the 14th century tower. The same exception was made when Plowman's building was demolished in 1896 under

19. Carfax Jack (in Museum of Oxford) formerly on Carfax Tower

the Carfax Improvement Scheme. Henry Hare, architect of Oxford Town Hall, wished to dress up the tower as a civic monument, but T.G. Jackson's much more conservative restoration (1897) was preferred, creating Carfax Tower as we know it today. The church clock was re-located on the tower in 1898 and modern replicas of 17th century quarter boys (figures holding axes) still attract attention when they strike the bells with their axes every quarter-hour. Hare had his way with other aspects of the Carfax improvement, designing Tower House (1896), now Crabtree and Evelyn, on one side of Carfax Tower and a new drapery store for Frank East (1896–7), now the HSBC, on the other side. The latter is built of ashlar stone and, according to

Pevsner, 'a lively design with all kinds of elements arranged in a random way'. There is a defunct drinking fountain at the south-east corner of Carfax Tower, provided by Ald. Tom Basson in 1923. Notice also the K2 phone box, placed here in the 1990s and a type not seen in Oxford before. Nearby, there used to be a blue police telephone pillar, which members of the public could use in an emergency. Above the stone gateway into the churchyard, leading now to a café, notice a fine copper bas relief of St. Martin tearing his cloak to give part to a beggar. This feature – also designed by Hare – was given to the city in 1896 by George Randell Higgins, the son of an Oxford wheelwright who had made his fortune as co-founder of the Peckham department store, Jones & Higgins. The old churchyard retains a few memorials, and, on the north-east buttress of the tower, one of the Peace Stones that celebrated the short-lived peace with

20. K2 Phone Box

21. St. Martin's plaque on archway

the conduit supplied piped water to some colleges and a few private houses; most citizens had to collect water from a lower cistern, unconcerned perhaps that their supply passed through the 'pizzle' of a carved ox! The City put wine in the conduit to celebrate special events such as the Restoration of Charles II in 1660. By 1637, Carfax Conduit was being criticized as an obstruction but it was only taken down in 1789. The City gave it to Lord Harcourt as an ornament in Nuneham Park where it is still to be seen.

France in 1814. This one was possibly dislodged during the demolition of Carfax Church, and carted away amongst the rubble. It was discovered in Old Marston churchyard in 1960 and reset here.

Carfax was the focus of Oxford's street markets until 1773–4, when traders were moved into the new Covered Market. On market days, this must always have been a hectic spot, and placing the immense Carfax Conduit (1615–7, John Clark?) in the central space where the city's main bullring had stood simply made matters worse. The highly decorative conduit was the most public part of a scheme conceived and paid for by Otho Nicholson (d.1622), which piped spring water from a well-house, which survives above North Hinksey. Nicholson, an elderly lawyer, seems to have been motivated, at least in part, by a wish to gain favour with James I, the king having taken a personal interest in an earlier London scheme. The upper cistern of

In September 1666, when everyone was on high alert following the Great Fire of London, a butcher drove his oxen across Carfax, encouraging them with cries of, 'Hiup! Hiup!' Worshippers in St. Martin's Church misheard this as 'Fire!' and hurried outside, some even claiming to smell smoke and burning pitch. On that occasion, there was no blaze to reshape the area, but Nicholas Hawksmoor produced unofficial proposals in around 1712 which sought to transform Carfax into a spacious Civic Forum adorned with statuary. Instead, the only contemporary improvement was the City's much more modest scheme, setting back the south-west corner in 1709–13 to form a colonnaded butter bench which replaced less adequate facilities at the Penniless Bench. The removal of the conduit freed up Carfax for stage coaches at the end of the 18th century but the railway stations generated growing local traffic from the 1850s and Oxford's horse tram network from 1881 included a cross-over at

Carfax. Increasing congestion encouraged the Carfax Improvement Scheme in 1896 and the setting-back of the north-east corner of Carfax in 1900–1. The rapid growth of motor traffic in the later 1920s brought chaos to Carfax, which now formed the junction between two major roads, the A34 and the A40. The south-west and south-east corners of Carfax were set back and rebuilt in a chaste historical style (1930–1, Ashley & Newman) to provide more space and even pedestrian subways were proposed in c.1930. Traffic lights were introduced in 1933 and the duty policeman who remained a feature of Carfax until the 1970s plunged boldly into the queues of vehicles when the need arose. Bypasses around Oxford, built between 1932 and 1965, gradually removed most of the through traffic from Carfax. Traffic management measures since the 1970s and particularly the closure of High Street to most vehicles during the day in 1999 have made Carfax once again a place where pedestrians choose to linger.

23. Bees Cartouche over main entrance to Lloyds Bank, 1-3 High Street

The attractive Lloyds Bank, on the north-east corner of Carfax (1900–3, Davey & Salter) was built in two stages, beginning with the High Street façade and then the corner into Cornmarket. It is an amazingly flamboyant building with large shaped gables and a delightful ship weathervane on the corner turret, which harks back to Lloyds maritime origins. The sumptuous carvings by an Oxford man, W.H. Feldon, include a beehive, the bank's former symbol, representing industry and hard work, above the main door and, on the upper floors, overflowing cornucopias which promise rich rewards to careful savers. Inside, the banking hall contains a replica of the Elizabethan plaster ceiling from the previous building on the site. The Cornmarket Street frontage originally had a separate ground floor shop occupied by the jewellers H. Samuel from c.1911 to 1921.

It's a long journey from the exuberant Lloyds Bank building back to the origins of High Street as one of the principal roads of the Saxon *burh*. Initially, High Street probably terminated at an east

24. Carved cornucopias on Lloyds Bank, 1-3 High Street

gate where St Mary the Virgin Church now stands, but Oxford's defences were extended eastwards in the early 11th century to a point near the present Eastgate Hotel. This extension created High Street's famous curve, noted by Wordsworth in his poem about 'the stream-like windings of that glorious street'. Houses and churches were built on both sides, and university halls and colleges began to appear among them in the 12th century. Leonard Hutten, in the 1620s, remarked that High Street was 'the fairest and longest streete of the Citty .. . continued, on both sides, with Cittizens Houses all the length'. He chose to overlook All Souls College and University College, but his description is a reminder that High Street was as much a Town as a Gown thoroughfare. The street was filled with stalls on market days in medieval times, and sellers of straw for thatching roofs occupied the centre of the road between All Saints' Church and the Eastgate. Pigs were sold outside All Saints' Church, now Lincoln College Library, until 1684, and butchers set up their

stalls between Carfax and Turl Street on market days until the 1770s. Following the Oxford Improvement Act of 1771, these obstructions were swept away, and High Street was paved by 1779, with stone pavements and side gutters replacing a central drainage channel. Especially at this end of High Street, former citizens' houses are still very evident, but many of the tall, timber-framed and jettied houses that so impressed Hutten have been rebuilt, hidden behind later facades or replaced by commercial, college or university developments. The overall result has been to create what Nikolaus Pevsner described as 'one of the world's great streets'.

Now cross with care to the south side of High Street and turn left to view properties on the other side. Lloyds expanded into nos. 4–5 High Street in 1976, a very different building retaining an ashlar stone façade dating from the late 18th or early 19th century. Old-established ironmongers, Gill & Ward, had a shop here between c.1846 and

25. Fragments of ceramic internal wall tiles from former Sainsbury's 4 High Street

1925 before crossing the street and later moving to premises in Wheatsheaf Yard. Sainsbury's opened their first Oxford grocery store at no. 4 in 1911, expanding into no. 5 in 1927 and this shop, complete with colourful tiled walls, flourished until the Westgate Centre opened in 1974. The late 18th century façades of nos. 6 and 7 were rebuilt in facsimile in 1958, the former having a fine neo-Classical Venetian window on the first floor. Edward Lock and his son, Sir Joseph Lock, were goldsmiths and bankers here between c.1772 and 1844 and no. 7 was then Underhill's grocery shop from c.1846 to 1921, before housing the International Stores until 1978. Jack Wills complemented these buildings with a fine traditional shop front in 2012. No. 8 High Street was redeveloped between the Wars and the continued expansion of Webber's department store further down led to the rebuilding of no. 9 (Whistles) in commercial neo-Georgian (1934, G. T. Gardner). Webber's department store (1905–71) grew out of the City Drapery Stores which began trading at no. 12 High Street in 1880 and soon took over nos. 10–11 (LK Bennett). The latter has a stuccoed 18th century front with rusticated quoins but a gable visible behind the parapet shows that this was a fashionable up-dating of an older property, not a complete rebuilding. The Georgian character of no. 12 (Pizza Hut) was radically altered when the entrance to Market Avenue 1 was cut through (1881) and bulky display windows were inserted on the two upper floors.

Nos. 13–16 High Street (1773–4, John Gwynn) were initially known as the New Parade. They have a three storey ashlar stone façade with a central moulded cornice and pedimented feature. With sash windows, retained only at no. 16, and small-paned shopfronts – long gone – they provided an impressive introduction to Gwynn's Covered Market and they were built to recoup part of the cost of that scheme, which spelled the end for street markets in Oxford. Webber's took over nos. 13–15 between the Wars and spoiled the building with a continuous shop fascia and plate glass windows but sympathetic reinstatement has since re-created much of its original character. Booksellers Slatter & Rose flourished at no. 16 from c.1901 to 1956 and upstairs rooms provided extra accommodation for the neighbouring Mitre Hotel. The Mitre was first recorded in about 1310 and the building's oldest feature is a 14th century cellar. It later became an important coaching inn and the south front of about 1630 was heightened and modernized in the late 18th century with stucco, canted bays and sash windows. The novelist, William Makepeace Thackeray, held a committee meeting in one of the ground floor rooms in July 1857 when he was seeking election as an Independent Liberal MP for Oxford. It was a hot day and the window was open, allowing a 'spy' outside to overhear him speaking in favour of the Sunday opening of museums and galleries. This opinion, gleefully broadcast, upset many potential supporters and Thackeray was

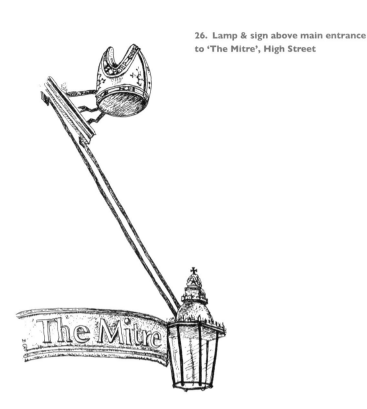

26. Lamp & sign above main entrance to 'The Mitre', High Street

subsequently defeated by the official Liberal candidate, Edward Cardwell. The building's 17th century moulded entrance doorway leads now into a restaurant since the upper floors of the hotel became student accommodation for Lincoln College in 1968. On the corner of High Street and Turl Street, notice a massive cast-iron lamp post (c.1895) with a two-branch fitting at the top. This is the only survivor of a type installed by the Oxford Electric Co., Ltd., when electric street lighting was introduced to the city centre.

Cross High Street at the pedestrian crossing and enter the Covered Market

by the Avenue 4 entrance, noticing colourful modern murals by Hugh Dunford-Wood. More can be seen in the entrances to Avenues 2 and 3. The original market (1773–4, John Gwynn) had colonnaded blocks of shops for butchers and poulterers and an open area near Market Street for other traders; it was also narrower, occupying the sites of the modern Avenues 2–4. The rear part of Avenue 1 where the roof is supported by stone piers and iron trusses was an extension of 1839–40 (Thomas Wyatt, junior). Avenue 1 was extended through to High Street in 1881 and the rest of the Market was rebuilt over the next two decades with high timbered

roofs (E. G. Bruton and others), providing over 150 shops and stalls. Many of these have now been amalgamated to form larger units and, although you can still find excellent butchers, greengrocers, a fishmonger, a delicatessen and a cheese shop here, the Covered Market today offers much more than food shopping. Watching cake decorators at work at The Cake Shop in Avenue 4 is endlessly fascinating!

Leave the Market at the north end of Avenue 1 and notice above the entrance the date stone 1897 marking the completion of the 19th century extension and rebuilding of the Covered Market. Across Market Street, notice the almost surreal contrast between the Gothic window of Jesus College Library and the former Marks and Spencer building. Now turn right and head for Turl Street, noting

27. Bears Mural by Hugh Dunford-Wood. Avenue 3

28 Central Cross Avenue roofs

29 Hayman's fish shop, Avenue 1

the rear elevation of Jesus College with its profusion of chimneys recalling the days of coal fires in every room. Beyond the rear wall of the Covered Market, Lincoln House (1938–9, G. T. Gardner) was a piece of sympathetic infilling on the site of Lincoln College stables. All the ground floor shops have small-paned shop fronts and the rough cast upper floors with bays and sash windows merge happily with properties round the corner.

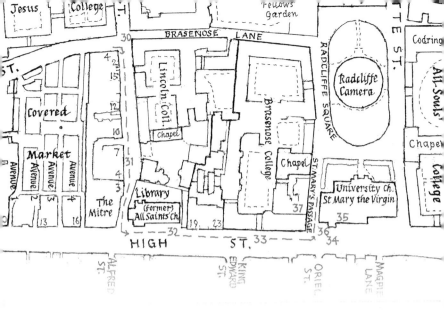

4 Turl Street to St Mary's Passage

As you reach Turl Street, notice a Lincoln Imp gazing down from a gable behind Lincoln College front. To your left, there is an old-style bracketed street light high up on the corner of Jesus College with a CCTV camera below mounted on an ornamental iron bracket; such is the attention to detail in modern Oxford! Glance across the road into Brasenose Lane, a narrow pedestrian thoroughfare which retains the central gutter once common to all streets. A medieval name, St. Mildred's Lane, recalls a church (c.1122–1427) on the site of the front quad of Lincoln College. Statues of St. Mildred (right) and the Virgin Mary by Stephen Cox (2009) fill two niches in the gate-tower of Lincoln College (founded 1427). The 15th century front (refaced

1824 and restored 1958) leads the eye down to the former All Saints' Church. Westward expansion of the church in medieval times caused the pronounced deviation of Turl Street at the southern end. Cross the road and look at some of the buildings on the west side of Turl Street. Beyond Lincoln House, no. 14 (The Missing Bean) is a three storeyed and timber-framed house of 17th century origin with a second floor jetty and two gables, supported by grotesque human brackets. Stucco masks the framing, and other alterations include 18th century sash windows, 19th century first floor bays, and a modern shopfront. No. 13 is typically 18th century and probably hides an older core behind its rough-cast timber-framed front. The next three houses and shops were formerly one

30. Looking east along Brasenose Lane to Radcliffe Square

building, occupied as the Maidenhead Inn from 1607 to 1899. The timber framing is typically disguised by rough cast and later windows but a continuous jetty is evident at second floor level and there are four gables above the cornice. Rowell & Son, jewellers in Oxford since 1797, have been at no. 12 since 1986 after moving from their High Street shop. Walters of Oxford, the tailors, occupy the rest of the Maidenhead building and the next property, a three storey timber-framed house with sash windows upstairs which probably dates from the 18th century. Walters – 'The Man's Shop', according to the projecting sign – was founded in c.1908 and the firm was noted between the Wars for supplying pith helmets, travelling baths and other necessities to Varsity men heading for the colonies.

The yard beyond Walters led to Mitre Hotel stables and outbuildings, rebuilt in half-timbered style to form the Turl Bar in 1926 and converted into the Turl Lecture Room and Seminar Rooms in 2011. Two 19th century buildings follow, a three storey stuccoed brick house, nos. 6 and 7, and the prominently gabled nos. 4–5. No. 6 has been the shop and workshop of Ducker & Son, the bespoke shoemakers, since 1867 and it has a fine shop front with good lettering. Ducker's are said to have made shoes for the German First World War fighter ace, Baron von Richthofen, but it was in fact the Red Baron's cousin, Wilhelm, who attended Oxford University as a Rhodes Scholar in 1913-14.

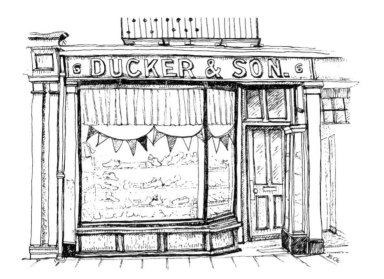

31. Ducker's shop front, 6 Turl St.

Back on the east side beyond the college façade, notice the lodgings of the Rector of Lincoln College (1930, Herbert Reed), an attractive stone building in neo-Georgian style on a site originally occupied by town houses. It was erected after the college failed to raise the money for a grandiose 1920s scheme involving a bridge across Turl Street to new buildings on the west side. The former All Saints' church (1706–9, Henry Aldrich; steeple 1718–20 by Aldrich and Nicholas Hawksmoor) provides a fitting architectural climax to the street. Described by Pevsner as 'one of the most perfect English churches of its date,' All Saints' has a projecting west tower topped by a rotunda and spire and it replaced the medieval church which had been largely destroyed by the collapse of the spire in 1700. After the demolition of St. Martin's Church in

1896, All Saints' became the City Church but it closed as a place of worship in 1971 and was cleverly converted into Lincoln College Library (1972–5, Robert Potter). Opposite the former church, no. 3 Turl Street is a 17th century three storey roughcast timber-framed house which has later sash windows upstairs and a casement window in the gable. The vaulted cellar dates from the 13th century. Booksellers occupied the ground floor shop for many years from 1906. Beyond this shop, you pass the side elevation of the Mitre where the sight of diners enjoying their meals may tempt you to consider a refreshment break. This range dates originally from the 17th century but has been modernized and in part heightened from three to four storeys.

Emerging into High Street, turn left

32. Former All Saints' Church now Lincoln College Library

past All Saints' Church. A robinia tree billows out into High Street from the former churchyard, a modern rival to the sycamore further down. A cabstand sign on the churchyard railings, now removed, recalled the All Saints' cab rank, which was in use from Victorian times until recent changes to city centre bus stops. Next come nos. 19–23 High Street, houses with early 19th century stuccoed and timber-framed fronts with sash windows. All but one have an eaves cornice and parapet, the exception being no. 22 (Scrivens, opticians) with a sashed dormer in a mansard roof. No. 23 (Footprints) was occupied by the tailor

33. Royal Arms above double doors High Street range, Brasenose College

James Embling between c.1846 and 1888 and, between c.1909 and 1968, by Ryman & Co., Ltd., well-known art dealers and printsellers who had previously been at nos. 24–5. The upper floors of these houses became student accommodation for Brasenose College between 1929 and 1934. Further on, the High Street front of Brasenose College (1887–1909, T. G. Jackson) displaced nos. 24–31, a range of shops and houses extending to St Mary's Passage. Edward Bracher was an early Oxford photographer at no. 26 High Street between c.1844 and 1865 and took on Henry Taunt as a general assistant in 1856, thus launching him into a life of photography. Brasenose had dreamed of expanding on to High Street since the 18th century and Jackson's

New Quadrangle finally achieved that long-term objective. His original scheme envisaged a steeple with an openwork 'crown' to rival the nearby spires of All Saints' and St. Mary's, but this was abandoned in favour of a traditional gate tower. The High Street façade is full of exuberant and high quality detail, including carved foliage on the parapets, grotesques above bay windows and a lion and a unicorn supporting the Royal Arms over the gateway.

Reaching St. Mary's Passage, you come to the probable eastern limit of the original Saxon *burh* laid out in c.910. The first East Gate would have stood here and it is argued that St. Mary's Passage, the former Schools Street, and Oriel Street across High Street represent the road that would have been formed inside the ramparts. Today's Catte Street and Magpie Lane echo the line of the defensive ditch outside the ramparts. St. Mary the Virgin Church is first recorded in 1086, but it seems likely that there was a Saxon church here occupying a similar position to the churches beside the North and South Gates in the town wall. That role would have ceased in the early 11th century when the defended area of Oxford was extended to a new East Gate where the Eastgate Hotel now stands.

Beyond a propped-up almond tree – a beautiful sight in early Spring – you come to the exuberant south porch of the church (1637, John Jackson) with its twisted columns and a sculpture of the Virgin and Child. Puritans saw the image as evidence of popery and iconoclastic Parliamentary soldiers shot the heads off the figures in 1642, but the damage was later repaired. St. Mary's Church became the University Church at an early date and its common bell summoned scholars as the one at St. Martin's roused the townsfolk. Congregation, the University's governing body, met in the church from at least 1252 and Congregation House (c.1320–7), facing Radcliffe Square, was the University's first purpose-built building with an upstairs room used as a library until the completion of Duke Humfrey's Library after 1480. The exterior claims attention, with its soaring spire (c.1315–25) and its pinnacled and buttressed chancel (1463) and nave and south aisle (c.1485–

34. Detail of south porch, St. Mary the Virgin Church

95). Inside, you find yourself in a spacious and well-proportioned nave lit by tall Perpendicular windows. Only the north aisle chapel built in c.1328 by Adam de Brome (d.1332), rector of St. Mary's and the founder and first Provost of Oriel College, survived this late 15th century rebuilding, albeit with new windows. Formerly St. Mary's Chapel, this is now known as the De Brome Chapel and it contains a reconstructed altar tomb with a 14th century lid which is traditionally ascribed to Adam de Brome. University ceremonies continued to be held in the church until the Sheldonian Theatre was completed in 1669 and, as we have seen, the city's annual St. Scholastica's Day humiliation took place here until 1859.

The Protestant Oxford Martyrs, Latimer, Ridley and Cranmer, were tried for heresy in the nave in 1555. Archbishop Thomas Cranmer was meant to make the submission here in March 1556 that would save his life. Instead, he dramatically confirmed his faith and walked to the stake 'with a firm step and a smiling countenance'. A modern plaque on the north wall of the nave records the names of all those, Protestant and Catholic, who were local martyrs of the Reformation in the 16th and 17th centuries. A Gothic stone screen and the organ mask the chancel, and pews in the nave focus the attention of the congregation on the pulpit. Charles and John Wesley preached here in the 18th century and so too did John Henry Newman when he was vicar between 1828 and 1843 and a leading light in the Oxford Movement. On the north wall of the nave, a large brass plaque recalls men of the Oxfordshire Light Infantry lost in a now almost forgotten imperial war in Beloochistan in 1885–6. A note at the entrance to the chancel records that German Lutheran services have been held in the church since September 1939. By this time, Oxford had many German and Austrian refugees from Nazi persecution who were of Jewish origin but were members of the Lutheran Church. Oxfam, originally the Oxford Committee for Famine Relief, was founded in the Old Library on October 5th, 1942, its initial aim being to relieve famine in Greece caused by the Allied naval blockade.

St. Mary's contains memorials to senior members of the University, such as David Gregory (d.1708), Savilian Professor of Astronomy, who is commemorated beside the south porch by a splendid bust and three *putti* with astronomical instruments. Many townsfolk are remembered too and, in the south aisle below the Gregory memorial, you'll find a floor slab commemorating Alderman John Nixon (d.1662), a wealthy mercer who was three times Mayor of Oxford and lived

35. Memorial to David Gregory, internal South Wall, St Mary the Virgin Church

in High Street opposite the church. He founded a school for 40 sons of freemen in 1658 and his memorial comments that 'with less noyse, farr greater bounties were disperst unknown'. Nearby, on the south wall, a poignant tablet recalls the death of Elizabeth Hanwell in 1787 a few days after the birth of her first child, Charlotte Elizabeth, who lived only six months.

Leaving St. Mary's, retrace your steps to St. Mary's Passage and head north towards Radcliffe Square. Notice in the shadow of the church a cast-iron pump, installed perhaps in the early 19th century, which would have served the parish before many houses had piped water. In medieval times, St. Mary's Passage was part of Schools Street, which continued

through to the city wall in Broad Street until the building of the Bodleian Library extension (1610–12). Beyond the church, the street was originally lined with houses, academic halls where students lived, and the schools or lecture rooms where they were taught. St. Mary's Entry, the timber-framed and gabled structure on your left, dates back to the 17th century and the property was effectively the University's printing house between 1585 and 1617. The University loaned Joseph Barnes (d. 1618), a bookseller and vintner, £100 in 1584 to establish a printing press and he printed some 300 books here before retiring with all but £20 of his loan repaid. The building later became the City Arms pub until it was converted, with neighbouring billiard rooms, into a private house (1884, Wilkinson & Moore). It has

37. Satyrs on porch and green man on door, Brasenose College

subsequently been much modernized to provide bursary offices and residential accommodation for Brasenose College. Note the two carved satyrs supporting the ornate door-hood and the green man panel in the door. This door is said to have inspired C. S. Lewis while writing his classic children's story, *The Lion, the Witch and the Wardrobe*, as the entrance to the magical world of Narnia. Beyond the jettied first floor which follows, Stamford House (1895, H.W. Moore)

replaced a 16th century building which had long been a grocer's shop. It has two elaborate timber gables above its ashlar stone elevation and the name recalls the brief migration of Oxford University to the more peaceable Lincolnshire town in the 13th century. The bronze sanctuary knocker which gave its name to the medieval Brasenose Hall was also taken to Stamford and was only reclaimed by the college in 1890.

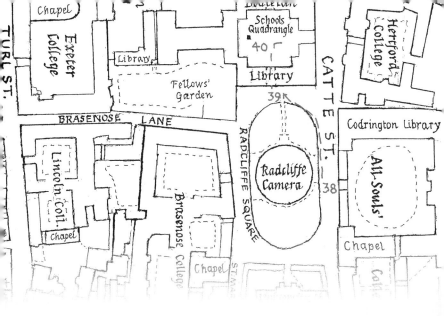

5 Radcliffe Square and Bodleian Library

Passing a retained lamp post with a Winsor lantern, you emerge into one of Oxford's finest views across Radcliffe Square, but chronologically it's worth keeping to the west side for the moment. Brasenose College was founded higher up the street in 1509 on the site of Brasenose Hall and began to expand southwards in the mid 17th century. You first come to the ashlar-faced chapel (1656–66, John Jackson). The east window has Gothic tracery, but there is a Classical open pediment above it and the building is finished off with an urn-topped parapet. The adjoining library (1657–64), again by John Jackson, was built over a cloister that had no windows on this side until the space was converted into rooms in 1807. On the upper floor, the Venetian

oriel window beside the chapel has matching thick garlands and decorative details. Further north, the library is lit by nine round-headed traceried windows below a restless crenellated roof-line interrupted by Classical pediments. Passing a doorway which features a cartouche of the Royal Stuart arms, you come to the Tudor frontage of the college, built between 1509 and 1518. As so often in Oxford, the college provided extra accommodation (c.1605–35) by adding a third storey to the Old Quad. The Radcliffe Square front is ornamented by attractive oriel windows and the Royal Tudor arms are displayed above the doorway of the panelled gate tower. Note the dragon and mastiff supporting the arms and the angels supporting the crown. Square-headed mullioned windows light the 17th century upper floor.

Brasenose originally fronted on to Schools Street, but its setting was radically altered in the 18th century. In around 1712, the architect Nicholas Hawksmoor prepared an unofficial town planning scheme for central Oxford which included a University Forum here to match the one he envisaged for the City at Carfax. His forum would have been virtually an empty square containing the odd column or statue. Given that there were still many small properties on both sides of School Street and Cat Street, it was an improbable ambition. The concept was realized in a very different form after John Radcliffe (1652–1714), Oxford graduate and Royal physician, left money in his will towards the building and endowment of a new library. Various sites were considered before the present one was chosen and James Gibbs' first design in 1735 was for a rectangular library. Hawksmoor proposed a domed circular structure before he died in 1736 and Gibbs was persuaded to adopt that scheme, going on to design the Radcliffe Camera (1737–,49), a lighter and much more Baroque building which is the glorious focal point of Radcliffe Square.

The Camera, so-called from the Latin word for a vaulted chamber, originally housed an upstairs science library approached through great open arches in the rusticated ground floor. The building was an unlikely venue for a grand royal banquet in June 1814 when the Prince Regent, the Tsar of Russia, the King of Prussia and Marshal Blücher visited Oxford after the Allies had seemingly defeated Napoleon. A few days later, a great dinner was held in Radcliffe Square for no fewer than 4,000 'poor but respectable' inhabitants of the city. Radcliffe Square was studded with stone bollards and taller obelisks topped by lamps in the early 19th century. Now, its cobbled street surface (re-laid 2005–7), one of the few remaining examples in Oxford, provides a perfect, though physically challenging, setting for all the grand buildings around the square.

A classic Oxford story has one or more drunken dons feeling their way round and round the Radcliffe Camera as they try in vain to find their way back to Brasenose on a dark night. This event must have occurred before 1827 when iron railings, designed by Henry Hakewill, were placed around the Camera to prevent undesirables from misusing the open ground floor. The Bodleian Library took over the Camera in 1862 and enclosed the ground floor arches to provide more space, creating a new entrance on the north side of the building. The railings around the Camera were removed as unfashionable in 1936, making it easier for an undergraduate to climb the building and place a small flag on the cupola in May 1937. The following month, another student returning to earth 'was confronted by Bodley's Librarian and four stalwart constables'. Replacement railings were installed in 1993 to keep young footballers and picnickers off the grass, proving an instant hit with the many cyclists looking for a secure parking place.

The tower and spire of St Mary the Virgin Church dominate the south side of Radcliffe Square. The tower was probably begun in the late 13th century and the Decorated Gothic spire dates from c.1315–25. Note the gabled pinnacles at each angle of the tower, which incorporate statues of saints and are enriched with ballflower ornament. Both the De Brome Chapel (c.1328) to the right of the tower and the Congregation House (c.1320–7) away to the left were remodelled externally in the 15th century to match the Perpendicular style of the rebuilt nave and chancel.

Walk across towards the North Quad of All Souls College (c.1716–34, Nicholas Hawksmoor) where there is an exquisite view of the twin towers through iron gates dated 1734. College Fellows had long felt cramped in their medieval buildings and Dr George Clarke first proposed expanding north across the site of the cloisters in about 1705. Such a grand scheme became possible in 1710 when Christopher Codrington, a former Fellow and West Indian sugar planter, left the college £6,000 to build a new library. Hawksmoor provided alternative designs in classical or Gothic style in 1715, and the Fellows opted for Gothic to match the 15th century chapel. In fact, Hawksmoor's Gothic was simply an exciting veneer for a quad which is symmetrical in its layout and contains buildings which are largely classical in proportion. Note, for example, the great west window of the Codrington Library which displays Gothic tracery to the outside world but forms a Venetian window inside, lighting a wholly classical interior.

Continue around Radcliffe Square, noticing Exeter College Fellows' Garden behind the high stone wall next to

38 Two heads from All Souls' iron gates facing Radcliffe Square

39. Radcliffe Square glimpsed from the passage to the Schools' Quadrangle

Brasenose Lane. A large horse chestnut tree known as Heber's Tree flourished at the corner of this garden until it had to be felled in 1990. It was so-called because it shaded the rooms of Reginald Heber (1783–1826), later Bishop of Calcutta, when he was at Brasenose College. The Bodleian Library Schools Quadrangle (1613–24) looms large to the north, presenting quite an austere façade. It is an ashlar stone building three storeys high with identical four-light windows to each floor, relieved at the top by battlements and pinnacles. To understand how it came to be here, you have to go back to the University's decision in the 1420s to build an impressive Divinity School for theology lectures on the west side of Schools Street. The master mason, Richard Winchcombe (d. 1439?), prepared designs for a grand single storey structure with large traceried windows, but work ground to a halt through lack of money. A new mason, Thomas Elkin, was appointed in 1440 to complete the building more cheaply without 'frivolous curiosities'. Humfrey, Duke of Gloucester (1390–1447), younger brother of Henry V and a patron of the arts, then complicated matters by donating much of his valuable library of classical texts to the University. In order to house this collection adequately, the University decided to add an upper floor to the Divinity School and the new library, known today as Duke Humfrey's Library, was opened to readers by 1466. Later, in 1480-3, the roof of the entire building was raised in order to allow construction

of a stunning stone vault, designed by the Oxford master mason, William Orchard (d. 1504), and the whole building was at last completed by 1490.

Most of the manuscripts in the University Library were lost or destroyed in the mid 16th century and the room was left empty and neglected. Thomas Bodley (1545–1613), returning to Oxford in 1598 after a diplomatic career, dedicated the last 15 years of his life to re-founding the library, aided by Sir Henry Savile (1549–1622), Warden of Merton College and a long-standing friend. Bodley proved to be an extraordinarily successful fund-raiser and he soon acquired a large and diverse collection of books through agents and adventurous book-buying expeditions across Europe. The Bodleian Library opened with 2,000 volumes in 1602 and, when James I visited the library in 1605, he was given a copy of the first printed catalogue of 6,000 books.

From the first in 1598, Bodley and Savile were planning an eastward extension to the university library across the site of Schools Street. This became crucial in 1610, when the Stationers' Company agreed to supply the library with a free copy of every book registered at Stationers' Hall, thus beginning the system of legal deposit in Britain. Walking through the archway into the Schools Quadrangle, you'll see the initial outcome away to your left – the Arts End extension over the Proscholium, a vestibule to the Divinity School, which was built in

40. Detail of Earl of Pembroke's statue

1610–12 by Halifax masons, John Akroyd and John Bentley, who had worked on Savile's family estates in Yorkshire and on the contemporary Fellows' Quadrangle at Merton College. The panelled façade and the window above the doorway were copied from the east front of the Divinity School and the skyline of battlements and pinnacles echoed that of the old library. A bronze statue of William Herbert, third Earl of Pembroke (1580–1630) by Hubert Le Sueur stands in front of the doorway. The Earl was an active Chancellor of the University from 1617–30 and

a generous benefactor to the Bodleian Library. The statue, originally at Wilton House, was given to the University in 1723.

Bodley clearly regarded Arts End as 'phase one' of a larger scheme and, in 1611, he set out to persuade the University to build a new quadrangle to the east which would replace all the 'ruinous little rooms' in the area which served as lecture and examination rooms. The initial plan was for a two storey building with schools on both floors – the names of

the ground floor schools are still painted in Latin above the doors – but Bodley left in his will the money to add a third storey for 'the stowage of books'. Akroyd and Bentley were again engaged as masons, but both were dead by 1615 and William Holt saw the building through to completion in 1624. Savile continued to supervise the work after Bodley's death and may well have designed the Tower of the Five Orders himself. The tower, described by Tyack as a 'gigantic piece of architectural pedantry', includes both Gothic pinnacles and classical columns which represent the fusion of old and new learning in the University. Note the sculptural group on the fourth floor (1620, John Clark), which shows a seated James I handing a copy of his writings to the kneeling University while Fame blows a celebratory fanfare on his trumpet. Leave the Schools Quadrangle by the vaulted archway under the tower and examine the original oak door on the way out. The moulded panels of the door contain the arms of the University and colleges founded before 1613 as well as the Royal Stuart arms and the Prince of Wales' feathers.

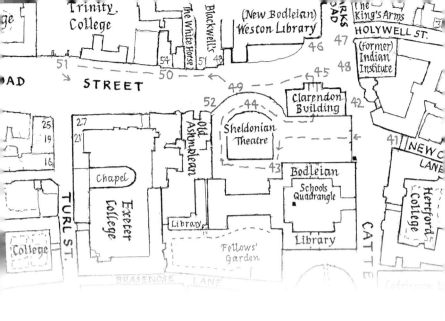

6 Catte Street to Broad Street

Emerging into Catte Street opposite Hertford College, we need to roll back the centuries to appreciate how much this area has changed. As we have seen, the street probably represents the line of the ditch outside the ramparts of early 10th century Oxford. It would then have been incorporated into the extended 11th century town as a road leading from High Street to Smith Gate, a postern in the town wall. The street was, for reasons unknown, called Cat Street from about 1200 until the 19th century; it then became Catherine Street but the present 'Olde English' spelling was adopted in 1930 to end confusion with the other Catherine Street in East Oxford. Catte Street has been much widened over the years. Houses on the west side were

demolished for the Schools Quadrangle in c.1613 and families made homeless were re-housed in Holywell Street. Further north, a huddle of buildings erected in the city ditch was cleared and the road was set back for the Clarendon Building in c.1711. Across the road, tall timber-framed houses stood in front of the north and south blocks of Magdalen Hall, now Hertford College (1820–2, E. W. Garbett), until they were demolished in about 1823. Perhaps people in some of these long-lost houses erected the maypole at the corner of Catte Street and New College Lane which is shown on Loggan's map of Oxford in 1675. Hertford (re-founded 1874) expanded rapidly and the north extension beyond New College Lane (1903–31, T. G. Jackson) is linked to the older college

41. Bridge of Sighs, Hertford College

buildings by a covered bridge, generally known as Oxford's Bridge of Sighs (1913–14, T. G. Jackson). Jackson had at first envisaged a below ground link between Hertford College and his North Quad before deciding on the bridge which must be one of Oxford's most photographed buildings. Beyond the bridge, the view is dominated by New College bell tower (1396–7), for which the use of stone from the Headington quarries was first recorded.

Hertford's North Quad claimed more town houses but Jackson incorporated and carefully restored the octagonal Chapel of Our Lady at Smith Gate (c.1520). Notice, above the south door, a sculpted representation of the Annunciation. This building had been converted into a house by 1583 and a shop by 1708 and it was sometimes, though wrongly, described as the oldest

house in Oxford. Holywell Press, founded in Holywell Street in c.1890, ran their printing and publishing business from the former chapel between c.1903 and 1921. The adjoining Smith Gate had a single archway, which was enlarged to take carts between 1635 and 1643, but it had been demolished by 1675.

Before leaving Catte Street, don't miss the listed red K6 phone box in the shadow of the Schools Quad. Sir Giles Gilbert Scott, architect of the nearby New Bodleian Library, was responsible for this English design icon in the 1930s. Now go through fine early 18th century wrought iron gates into the gravelled area between the north range of the Bodleian Library's Schools Quadrangle (1613–24), the Sheldonian Theatre (1663–9, Christopher Wren) and the Clarendon Building (1711–15, Nicholas Hawksmoor). Oxford's medieval town wall crossed

42 'Annunciation' stone carving, Chapel of Our Lady at Smithgate

this space and its course is marked by two parallel lines across the stone paving. The sharp north-eastward deviation of the wall at this point is thought to reflect the extension of Oxford's walled area in the early 11th century. Keep this history in mind as you savour the rich array of University buildings that now occupy the site. Bearing left around the corner of the Schools Quadrangle, glance up at the renewed grotesques (2009) at second floor level. These are based on designs inspired by children's books following a competition organized by the Oxford Preservation Trust. You are now in a magical, if slightly confined, courtyard between the Divinity School and the Sheldonian Theatre which has hardly changed since the 1670s. The Divinity School and Duke Humfrey's Library were completed after many years by 1490, forming a rectangular building five bays long which originally stood on the west

side of Schools Street and just inside the town wall. Its panelled buttresses, battlements and pinnacles helped to inspire the design of Bodley's new

43. Two grotesques: Sir Thomas Bodley & 3 Men in a boat (to say nothing of the dog) Bodleian Library

44. Detail of trophy carvings, North elevation. Sheldonian Theatre

buildings in the early 17th century. Notice the large six-light windows to the Divinity School and the smaller windows upstairs lighting the library bays. The projections at either end of the Divinity School are later additions, the one to the east being the Proscholium and Arts End extension of 1610–12. The matching extension at the other end (1632–7) contains the Chancellor's Court and Convocation House on the ground floor and the Bodleian Library's Selden End above. Convocation House took the University's governing body out of St. Mary's Church at last, and Parliament met in the room in 1665 and 1681 when there were outbreaks of plague in London.

By 1662, when William Sheldon, Archbishop of Canterbury, provided the money for a building for university ceremonies, Oxford's town wall was redundant and decayed. The Sheldonian Theatre (1663–9, Christopher Wren) replaced this section and extended back across the town ditch to Broad Street. It was Wren's first architectural work and Oxford's first classical building, based on the Theatre of Marcellus at Rome. This south elevation is the impressive main façade, crowned by a huge pediment, which faces the Divinity School – a splendid robing room on ceremonial occasions. A Gothick north doorway (1669, Christopher Wren?) was inserted in the older building to provide the necessary link with the new one. Continuing round the Sheldonian, notice the ashlar stone wall with niches, vases and a pedimented doorway, which separates this courtyard from Exeter College. The wall is punctuated by the side elevation and ceremonial entrance of the Old Ashmolean Building (1679–83, Thomas Wood), which we will consider later. An identical boundary wall at the other side of the Sheldonian, extending from Broad Street to the Schools Quadrangle, was removed when the Clarendon Building was erected. The Sheldonian Theatre effectively turns its back on Broad Street but the semi-circular north elevation is hugely distinctive and, as Tyack has commented, 'strangely reminiscent of the stern of a ship'. From here, you have good views into Broad Street over a stone screen topped with herms – human heads on plinths derived from Roman architecture – which are popularly known as the Emperors' Heads.

The Sheldonian Theatre initially accommodated the University Press as well as university ceremonies. The printing presses were located in the basement, compositors and editors worked in rooms under the galleries and books were stored in the attics. The bookstore was lit by a series of oval dormer windows 'so contrived that they admit air and exclude rain'. These were, unfortunately perhaps, removed before the present cupola (1837–8, Edward Blore) replaced Wren's elegant original. The Sheldonian Theatre houses the annual Encaenia ceremony when the University awards honorary degrees to famous people. With its fine woodwork and ceiling paintings by Robert Streater (1621–79), the building also provides a spectacular setting for concerts. Handel gave a series of concerts at the Sheldonian in 1733 and Haydn conducted his Symphony no. 92, nicknamed the Oxford, here when he received an honorary degree in 1791.

The University Press soon outgrew the Sheldonian and acquired prestigious new premises next door in the Clarendon Building (1711–15, Nicholas Hawksmoor), which remained its home until 1828. This grand building, inspired again by the architecture of ancient Rome, served also as a formal entrance to Oxford as a seat of learning. Built on the cleared site of houses built in the town ditch, it was partially funded by sales of Lord Clarendon's *History of the Great Rebellion*, published in 1702–4. Note his statue by Francis Bird (1721) in a niche facing you and glance up to see the lead statues of the Muses on the pediments (1717, Sir James Thornhill but two of the statues are fibre-glass replicas by Richard Kindersley installed in 1974) as you walk round to the north side of the building. The original statues were brought by river from London, and sat on the wharf at Folly Bridge for two years awaiting payment. Now turn left down the vaulted passageway towards Broad Street, recalling perhaps that the University controlled night policing in Oxford from this building until 1869. Erring citizens as well as students were likely to find themselves imprisoned in basement cells.

You emerge on the steps opposite the

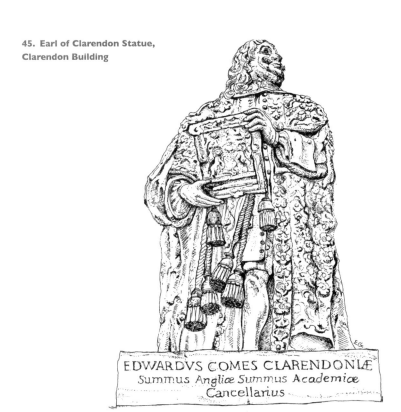

EDWARDVS COMES CLARENDONIÆ
Summus Angliæ Summus Academiæ
Cancellarius

New Bodleian Library (1937–40, Sir Giles Gilbert Scott), which required the demolition of 13 houses dating mostly from c.1600–50. By the 1930s, the Bodleian was running out of space and, after some debate, the University chose to locate a new building here rather than move the library to a less central location as Cambridge did. Scott's vast steel-framed structure encased in squared rubble stone appealed neither to modernists nor to traditionalists. Jan Morris remarked that it 'looks like a well-equipped municipal swimming bath, and replaced a nice corner of jostling old houses ...' Formerly criticized as a mere fortress of books, the building has been transformed (2011–15, Wilkinson Eyre Architects) following a benefaction from the Garfield Weston Foundation, and, as the Weston Library, it now draws in visitors through a new Broad Street entrance to view displays of the Library's treasures. The Bodleian's Special Collections are also conserved, housed, and made available to readers here. The ceremonial door on the corner was a scene of huge embarrassment in 1946 when the key broke in the lock during the official opening by King George VI;

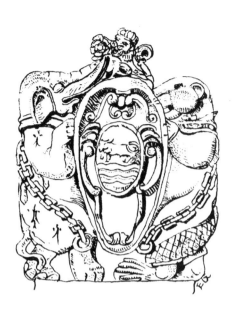

wisely perhaps, this door remains closed in the new era!

The jostling houses which the New Bodleian replaced included nos. 40–1 Broad Street, the home of Dr Henry Acland (1815–1900), Regius Professor of Medicine from 1857 to 1894, and the Coach and Horses pub on the corner of Parks Road. The Coach and Horses was originally known as the Prince's Arms as opposed to the King's Arms Inn founded in 1607 on the opposite corner. The latter was re-fronted and much altered in the 18th century and retained Oxford's last men only bar into the 1970s; today, the whole establishment seems popular with both sexes! Across Holywell Street, the vista down Broad Street is completed by the former Indian Institute (1883–96, Basil Champneys). Note the elephant and howdah weathervane and the

statues of Hindu gods on the corner. The Indian Institute replaced a fine early 18th century building similar in style to Vanbrugh House in St. Michael's Street. It was a coffee house from c.1762 to 1843, but was probably built for the eminent Oxford clockmaker, John Knibb (1650–1722), who was Mayor of Oxford in 1698 and 1710. The Oxford Martin School, established in 2005 with the daunting task of tackling major global challenges, took over the Indian Institute building in 2013 after extensive refurbishment.

The Clarendon Building steps provide an excellent view along Broad Street. Car parking currently adds some visual clutter but temporary obstructions were not unknown in the past. In September 1723, an extraordinary smoking contest took place on a temporary stage opposite the Sheldonian. A prize of 12 shillings was

47. Elephant & howdah weather vane, former Indian Institute

48. Hindu god term, former Indian Institute

promised to any man or woman who could smoke three ounces of tobacco without drinking or going off the platform. The eventual winner was an old soldier who smoked his ration 'gently' and was said to have had another four or five pipes the same evening. During the 1754

election, wooden polling booths filled the centre of the road from the old Ashmolean Museum to Turl Street.

Blackwell's world-famous bookshop occupies the first properties beyond the New Bodleian Library. Benjamin Henry

49. Blackwells & The White Horse public house Broad St.

Blackwell established his bookshop at no. 50 in 1879 and soon expanded next door into no. 51. They were originally a single building dating from the early 18th century and the front features rusticated quoins, an eaves cornice and pedimented dormers in the roof. The louvred shutters at all the upstairs sash windows are an attractive feature. Blackwell's also occupies nos. 48–49 Broad Street, which was built in cheerful 18th century style (1937–8, F. E. Openshaw) after the original property was undermined by demolition work next door. Behind these deceptively small premises, the underground Norrington Room (1966, Maguire and Murray) was built to house 160,000 books on 2½ miles of shelving. The White Horse pub at no. 52 is a modern 18th century style re-fronting of a 16th or 17th century structure with a bar front to the ground floor. No. 53 Broad Street was rebuilt in 1967 and the four storey 18th century front with bays is in fact a replica.

Kettell Hall (c.1620), beyond no. 53, deserves closer study, being a fine – and genuine – Jacobean house of coursed stone and three storeys high with mullioned windows and gables. Three gables face the street, the middle one being brought forward to form a projecting porch with a fine original door. It was built for Ralph Kettell, President of Trinity (1599–1643), who was noted for shearing off his students' long hair and peering through keyholes to check that they were working. He did ensure, however, that Trinity offered good beer so that they would be less likely to go out 'on the town'! Continuing west, you have a view through railings and past a lavender garden to the Jacobean style Front Quadrangle of Trinity College (1883–7, T.G. Jackson). Jackson had proposed a much larger scheme in 1880 which would have extended this range right up to the street, and replaced the 17th century Trinity Cottages with an ornate gateway. Defending the cottages,

50. Door Knocker on Kettell hall, Trinity College

William Morris argued that they were 'in their way as important as the more majestic buildings to which all the world makes pilgrimage'. Remarkably, the college decided to retain the rubble stone and timber-framed cottages and converted them into undergraduate rooms, initiating a welcome trend in the re-use of historic houses, which became more common in the 20th century. One early occupant, Hugh Legge, was less enthusiastic, remarking that 'I have to bend double going upstairs & can touch the roof of my bedroom with my head'. The façade of the cottages was restored and refaced in stucco (1968–9, Pinckheard & Partners) when the building was rebuilt to provide a porter's lodge and undergraduate rooms. Whereas Balliol College fronts decisively on to Broad Street, the principal buildings of Trinity College (founded as Durham College 1286; re-founded 1555) are much more reticent, and the ornamental gates opposite the end of Turl Street – a donation by Lord North in 1737 – lead the eye down through a garden to the

51. Main Iron Gates at Trinity College

52. Three of the Emperors' Heads from the screen wall outside the Sheldonian Theatre & Old Ashmolean

College chapel (1694, Dr Henry Aldrich in consultation with Christopher Wren). This was a revolutionary building in its day, the first Oxford chapel not to be built in a derivative Gothic style.

Where better to finish this walk than beside the Emperors' Heads outside the Sheldonian Theatre and the Old Ashmolean? The Old Ashmolean (1679–83, Thomas Wood), now the Museum of the History of Science, was a multi-purpose structure, housing the collection of natural curiosities which Elias Ashmole presented to the University in 1677 and teaching rooms for the University's School of Natural History. England's first chemical laboratory was located in the basement. Robert Plot (1640–96), Professor of Chemistry, was the first curator and he arranged for Ashmole's collection to be transported from London to Oxford by Thames barge in 1683 prior to the opening of the building by James, Duke of York, the future James II. As at the Sheldonian, the inspiration for the design was classical and the ashlar stone building presents a dignified frontage to Broad Street. Beneath a balustraded parapet, there are two rows of large windows and a central doorway approached by steps across the basement area. The curtain wall to the north followed the Sheldonian precedent and is adorned with Emperors' Heads, the present ones (1972, Michael Black) being the third set. The 17th century originals by the Oxford stone-carver William Bird were replaced by copies in 1868, but these were already seriously eroded when Max Beerbohm described 'great beads of perspiration glistening on the brows of those Emperors' as they witnessed the arrival of the *femme fatale*

Zuleika Dobson in his 1911 novel. Pevsner had wished to keep the 'ragged regiment' of Victorian heads because of their picturesque value and Oxford has seen many similar arguments between conservers and restorers. There have been many battles too between people favouring an Oxford of grand vistas and those preferring more intimate views. In 1667, the vista party won the argument when the University purchased and demolished a row of 17th century houses in the centre of Broad Street to reveal the new Sheldonian Theatre. Perhaps, in the near future, this fine view will be further enhanced as Broad Street becomes less of a highway and more a public realm.

Notes and Further Reading

Sally Alexander, *St Giles's Fair 1830-1914* (1970)

Donald Barnie, *Seventy-five Years' Co-operation in Oxford and District* (1947)

John Blair, *Frewin Hall: A Norman Mansion and a Monastic College*, Oxoniensia 43 (1978)

Brazen Nose (1977, 1980)

M.G. Brock and M.C. Curthoys, *History of the University of Oxford, vol. 7, part 2* (2000)

H. J. Butterfield, *Hill, Upton & Co., Notes on the history of the firm* (1924)

Don Chapman, *Oxford Playhouse* (2008)

Edmund Chillenden, *The Inhumanity of the King's Prison-Keeper at Oxford* (1643)

Andrew Clark, ed, *Survey of the Antiquities of the City of Oxford by Anthony Wood*, 3 vols., Oxford Historical Society 15, 17, 37 (1889-99)

Howard Colvin, *Unbuilt Oxford* (1983)

H.J. Compton, *The Oxford Canal* (1976)

G.V. Cox, *Recollections of Oxford* (1868)

Alan Crossley, *Victoria History of the County of Oxford, vol. 4: the City of Oxford* (1979)

C. H. Daniel, *Worcester College* (1900)

Mark Davies and Catherine Robinson, *A Towpath Walk in Oxford* (2001)

Brian Durham, *Oxford's Northern Defences: archaeological studies, 1971-1982*, Oxoniensia 48 (1983)

Dorothy Eagle and Hilary Carnell, *The Oxford Literary Guide to the British Isles* (1977)

Charles Fenby, *The Other Oxford* (1970)

Richard Foster, *F Cape & Co. of St Ebbe's Street, Oxford* (1973)

C.E. Goad, *Oxford City Shopping Centre plans*, revised 1995-7

Cliff Goodwin, *Inspector Morse Country* (2002)

Malcolm Graham, On Foot in Oxford no. 1: Gloucester Green and Jericho (1988)

Malcolm Graham, On Foot in Oxford, no. 9: North-West of Carfax (1980)

Malcolm Graham, *Oxford City Apprentices, 1697-1800*, Oxford Historical Society New Series 31 (1987)

Malcolm Graham, *The Oxford Reader: 150 Years of Oxford Public Libraries* (2004)

Malcolm Graham, *Oxfordshire at War* (1994)

Malcolm Graham, *The Suburbs of Victorian Oxford* (1985)

Christopher Hibbert, *The Encyclopaedia of Oxford* (1988)

R.D. Hill, *A History of St Edward's School 1863-1963* (1962)

M.G. Hobson & H.E. Salter, *Oxford Council Acts 1626-1665*, Oxford Historical Society 95 (1933)

Herbert Hurst, *Oxford Topography*, Oxford Historical Society 39 (1899)

K. Hylson-Smith, *A History of St. Giles' and the St. Cross/Pusey House site* (1993)

E.M. Jope, *The Clarendon Hotel. Oxford. Part 1: the site*, Oxoniensia 29 (1958)

Ian Ker, *John Henry Newman: a biography* (1988)

L. J. Kreitzer, *Oxford's First Quaker meeting place*, Oxoniensia 73 (2008)

Arthur Ledger, *A History of 100 Years Co-operation in Oxford* (1972)

Mary Leslie, *Through Changing Scenes* (1972)

P. J. Marriott, *Early Oxford Picture Palaces* (1978)

P. J. Marriott, *Oxford Pubs Past and Present* (1978)

Ian Meyrick, *Oxfordshire Cinemas* (2007)

Julian Munby, *Oxford Castle Medieval and Later buildings* (2000),

Julian Munby, *Zacharias', or the New Inn*, in Oxford Preservation Trust, 60th report for 1986 (1986)

Julian Munby and Hugh Walton, *The Building of New Road*, Oxoniensia 55 (1990)

Sir Charles Oman, *Castles* (1926)

Philip Opher, *Twentieth Century Oxford Architecture* (1995)

Anson Osmond, *Building on the Beaumonts: an example of early 19th century housing development*, Oxoniensia 49 (1984)

Oxford Archaeology, *Oxford Castle, Canal and College* (2008)

Oxford Archaeology, *Oxford Castle: a Heritage Survey* (1996)

Oxford Castle Heritage Project (2004)

Oxford City Council, *Gloucester Green Discussion*

Paper (1979)

Oxford City Council, *Gloucester Green: Development of Bii Option* (1980)

Oxford City Council, *Westgate Oxford* (c.1970)

Oxford City Fire Brigade, *Annual Report* (1966/7)

Oxford Dictionary of National Biography

Oxford Mail, *Fifty years of service: City Motors 1919-69* (1969)

Oxford Mail, *City Motors 60th Anniversary* supplement (1979)

Oxford Preservation Trust, *Annual Reports* (1945-6, 1951-2, 1986)

W.T. Pike & Co., *Views and Reviews Special Edition Oxford* (1897)

Bernard Reaney, *The Class Struggle in 19th Century Oxfordshire* (1970)

David Reed and Philip Opher, *New Architecture in Oxford* (1974)

John Rhodes, *Oxford Castle Conservation Plan* (1999)

Andrew Saint, *Three Oxford Architects*, Oxoniensia 35 (1970)

H. E. Salter, *Survey of Oxford*, 2 vols., Oxford Historical Society New Series 14, 20 (1960-9)

H. E. Salter, *Surveys and Tokens*, Oxford Historical Society 75 (1923)

Scott Wilson Kirkpatrick & Partners, *Oxford Central Area Study* (1968)

Jennifer Sherwood and Nikolaus Pevsner, *Oxfordshire* (1974)

A Short Memoir of Algernon Barrington Simeon MA (1929)

T. W. Squires, *In West Oxford* (1928)

V.E. Stack, ed., *Oxford High School 1875-1960* (1963)

The Story of the Acland Home, 1882-1958 (1958)

Victor Sugden, *Oxford Diary* (c.1993)

Taphouses: the Story of a Music Shop 1857-1957 (1957)

Thames Valley Archaeological Services, *Kendrew Quadrangle Excavations , phases 1-3* (2008)

William Tuckwell, *Reminiscences of Oxford* (1900)

Geoffrey Tyack, *Oxford: an Architectural Guide* (1998)

E.J. Warr, *The Oxford Plaque Guide* (2011)

H. Webb, *Medieval and Post-medieval Graveyard of St Peter le Bailey*, Oxoniensia 74 (2009)

J. P. Wells, *Martyrs' Memorial*, Oxford Magazine, 2.2.1968

W.R. Williams, *Parliamentary History of the County of Oxford* (1899)

Edward Wirley, *The Prisoner's Report* (1642)

www.annabelinda

www.ashmolean.org

www.oxfordshireblueplaques.org.uk

www.dianabell.co.uk

www.headington.org.uk

www.imagesofengland

www.leefitzgerald.co.uk/portfolio

www.oxford.gov.uk/planningapplications

www.oxfordpreservation.org.uk/projects/ memorial

www.rickmather.com

www.wikipedia

www.wiseabroad.com

A fully referenced copy of the text of this Oxford Heritage Walk can be viewed at www.oxfordpreservation.org.uk

NOTES AND FURTHER READING